Mary Dyer's Hymn
and Other Quaker Poems

Stanford Searl

D1342961

A Publication of The Poetry Box®

Cover Photograph of Quaker Martyrs Monument on Shelter Island,
    New York by Rebecca Warren Searl
Editing & Book Design by Shawn Aveningo Sanders.
Cover Design by Robert R. Sanders.

ISBN: 978-1-948461-36-8
Printed in the United States of America.

Published by The Poetry Box®, 2019
Beaverton, Oregon
ThePoetryBox.com

Dedicated to Santa Monica Quakers

Contents

Introduction

In the 1650's, the leaders of the Massachusetts Bay Colony responded with both fear and violence to the newly forming Children of the Light called "Quakers" in derision, assuming that this radical sect carried insurrectionary diseases that might infect the common people with sin and error – like a virulent virus in the body and soul. Hence, when Quakers started to arrive in Boston, both in 1656 and 1657, these dangerous, heretical Quakers were met with fines and imprisonment; they were stripped, whipped and jailed and their books and pamphlets were burned by the official executioner. In 1658, the Massachusetts General Court passed a law that said that any Quaker found in the Colony would be banished upon pain of death.

Hence, on October 27, 1659, two Quaker men were taken to the public scaffold (on or near Boston Common) amid noisy drumming from 200 soldiers (to drown out heretical speech) because they resisted banishment and thus, William Robinson and Marmaduke Stevenson were hanged and tossed into a common grave. At that same time, Mary Dyer, a fellow Quaker, was led up to the scaffold but reprieved at the last moment. However, after spending the winter of 1659-1660 at Shelter Island among other Quakers, including Cassandra and Lawrence Southwick (who were banished from Boston earlier), Mary Dyer returned to Boston in May of 1660 and was hanged in Boston June, 1660. In addition, a fourth Quaker, William Leddra, was hanged in March of 1660 in Boston.

All four of these Quakers were hanged because they were "convicted" of being dangerous, heretical Quakers (see the poem, "The Choke Weeds" in this collection) and because they refused to remain banished from the Colony. These poems explore some of the meanings of these Quaker prophets and martyrs in various songs and poems.

Based upon historical sources, scholarship and narratives of Quaker Sufferings, these poems engage imagination and memory to explore how some of these 17th century experiences may speak to readers today.

Quaker Martyrs Monument on Shelter Island, New York
(Photo by Rebecca Warren Searl)

Shelter Island Quaker Monument

Memory pulses through the granite slab
chanting broken bodies
sinking into dreams of Quaker names.
Tidal salt-water inlets fill up

with blue crabs, gone bottoms-up
smelling decay, rotting claws on the beaches
writing sandy letters inscrutable.
My nails and fingers scratch at moist sand,

those etched inscribed names
lost. Winds and rains washed out
nearly every name like
raised letters in ancient illuminated books.

Trowel-in-hand with watery half-gallons,
I tamp potting soil around rose stalks
surrounding the hard monument,
my fingers pricked by thorns

as dark blood oozes out onto the ground,
mixed with tears etching my cheek,
the stalks deposited in the new earth.
I feel my breathing slow,

waiting, turning away
from the foamy wash of history and decay
holding still and silent today.

Quaker Hymn

"People sing to feel part of something bigger than themselves,
which can be good, or can be very bad"
—George Benjamin, Composer
(in a *New Yorker* profile, September 17, 2018)

Because Quakers typically don't sing
at all it may seem absurd
that I, a Quaker poet,
search for suitable tunes.

I access melodies,
chants of suffering, doom and Light
hidden in plain sight—yet reserved for prophets—
entrances obscured, opaque, inaccessible.

I pray for a hymn to enter me,
leading my poet's heart and soul more deeply
like the second verse of "Holy Spirit, Truth Divine,"
words by the poet Longfellow's younger brother

to music by Louis Gottschalk.
The tune plays within me,
sliding out of my tenor voice
to proclaim "perish self in thy pure fire"

in the key of B flat major.
Top notes climb up the scale to dotted rhythms
a vocal prayer for love to glow within the singer,
resonant, urging a dissolution of self,

elemental notes taking the singer beyond words,
melodies that can't be said
carried along in the diaphragm,
musical pulses carrying the perishing self to the final cadence.

Openings

Neither awake nor dreaming,
I fell into an extended well
traveling into oddly marked familial roots
become a channel for memory,

drifting down to Mnemosyne herself.
I floated down and down,
submerged, suspended yet clear,
an openness to memory's figures

dredging 17th century gravely soil
now led beneath sleep and dreaming
into leaky roots,
absorbing family blood,

carrying genetic history from
my 9th great-grandfather, Richard Waterman,
a Proprietor in Rhode Island's founding,
friend, colleague, fellow conspirator with Roger Williams

as they walked over growling wolf pits,
ice crystals crusting footprints
as grandfather Waterman and Roger Williams
flee into a northeast blizzard,

footpaths disappearing in white-outs,
two heretics pushing through drifts and winds
to burrow next to the great Narragansett Bay,
ice formed on both beards as they slide into Rhode Island's icy haven.

Grandfather Waterman Speaks

Sanctified by God and the New Testament,
righteous Puritans came to kill and destroy,
purging the bodies and souls of Narragansetts,
burning an entire Pequot village,

stripping, whipping and hanging Quakers,
scourging the Massachusetts wilderness
of native people as if they were wolves,
exterminated for bounty.

God-fearing men of the Bible
brought plague and disease
like daily hurricanes of fiery winds,
a deep swath of howling and destruction.

These Puritans come into my mind
like a fearful hallucination
awash in hot blood,
a fever in body and brain

bringing me into the midst of Anne Hutchinson
and her prophetic ministry
as she claimed in the trial
immediate revelation of God through Biblical types.

Massachusetts ministers said she defied authority
and her error was to have been husband not wife,
a preacher and never a hearer
and worst, a magistrate and not a subject.

At her trial she said
only by the Lord's prophetical office
could she open scripture—never by herself
but Puritan men found her

immersed in the spirit of prophecy,
hearing divine voices—from Satan
yet wrapped up in scriptural texts and types
so, they banished her from the Colony.

Distant, yet ringing in sweetness,
my grandfather's voice enters, absorptive, playing changes
sounding like cries from the wilderness itself.

Memory

I found myself on a moist, sandy beach,
an island in the middle of Narragansett Bay,
awash in summertime tidal flats.
I splashed into the water, pushed ashore by the current

and heard guttural chanting,
calling to my heart and soul,
a chorale, organ-like fugue
singing of suffering, awakening, dissent and love.

Bach's Goldberg variations played,
ornamented yet driving and melodic at once,
a churning, rhythmic counterpoint,
the ornaments spinning out of Glenn Gould's imagination

leading back to the opening theme in variation thirty-two,
but now associated with another theme,
from Roger Williams' *A Key into the Language of America*,
openings into Narragansett native language

to offer multiple keys,
creative, forming and reforming,
to carry across centuries to my grandfather Waterman,
friend, confident, wolf-hunter and fellow dissident

guide and advisor
through dreams and hallucinations.
I dropped into this world of the 1630's Massachusetts Bay Colony
and eavesdropped on grandfather Waterman

as I listened how Williams lived and traded with Narragansetts
as he became a listening minister
squeezed by uncomfortable truths in the heart
engorged by a surprising intimacy with native sachems.

Roger Williams and His Keys to America

Banished by his English brethren,
he followed in Narragansett footsteps
walking into well-heads of hidden streams

like bubbling rivulets of grace
flowing out of the hills and valleys
running out into muddy tidal flats

where Narragansett Bay's salty freshness filled his soul
and underground springs swirled around his feet
and came to him, singing

> *The wild Barbarians with no more*
> *Then Nature, goe so farre:*

> *If Natures Sons both wild and tame,*
> *Humane and Courteous be:*
> *How ill becomes it Sonnes of God*
> *To want Humanity?*

Translation turned into discovery
as preacher became poet
openings into Narragansett mysteries

materials from rude lumps at sea
as he formed and reformed
now author as iron-monger

who cast multiples keys
in this house of discovery
like Peter in Matthew with keys from Christ.

This new mode of Christian colonization
undercut conversion, translated as a heretic,
cast out by the Massachusetts General Court

yet with the Narragansetts in continual dialog.

> *Boast not proud English, of thy birth & blood,*
> *Thy brother Indian is by birth as Good.*
> *Of one blood God made Him, and Thee & All,*
> *As wise, as faire, as strong, as personall.*

> *By nature wrath's his portion, thine no more*
> *Till Grace his soule and thine in Christ restore,*
> *Make sure thy second birth, else thou shalt see,*
> *Heaven ope to Indians wild, but shut to thee.*

This minister poet pleaded for all humanity
from exiled Providence, sympathetic to the heathens
who grow in grace and stature in these

odd translations, where body and soul
meet the underlying secrets of native peoples,
feasting upon welcome and love in his banishment.

The Choke Weeds

The Massachusetts General Court said that Quakers burned Bibles,
Denied scriptures and preached heaps of nonsense.
Quakers were parasitic weeds that choked healthy herbs and scrubs,
Attaching to the roots of family and state,
Possessed by Satan as with the Indians.

They were secret Catholics and witches,
Infused by the sin of Pride
Like Quaker Cassandra Southwick of Salem
Who said she was "greater than Moses,
For Moses had seen God but twice,
His bad side only but she had seen him
Three times and face to face."

Deluded Quakers had abandoned their families
Become heretic vagabonds, roaming and wandering
Without a settled home, tangled up,
Insistent perfectionists, denying original sin itself
Bringing error, anarchy and disorder to the Commonwealth,
Threatening to infect the entire community.

Puritan rulers mutilated, scarred these Quakers
With cuts, bruises, beatings and insults,
Chopping off the ears of some Quaker men,
Stripping and whipping both men and women,
Withholding light and food.

The executioner hanged four Quakers,
Including one woman, Mary Dyer
Because they refused to be permanently banished
And because they were licentious, heretical Quakers.

The Soul

"In short, the element that most separates modern observers from
seventeenth-century religious visionaries is the simple but profound
fact that they believed in the soul and we, in our scholarly roles as
social scientists, historians, or literary critics, do not."
—Phyllis Mack, *Visionary Women*

I searched for a secret theme,
one that could unlock the Quaker soul
and open their obsessive erasures of the self,
some revealing keys into their hearts and souls.

But how could I uncover my own prophetic voice
to enter into this world of the Lamb's war and Quaker prophecy?
Did I need to take a first step and believe in the reality of the soul
and possess a burning inward desire to empty-out all flesh?

Could I possibly follow the secret clue
dropped by Richard Farnsworth how
"I am a white paper Book
without any line or sentence

but as it is revealed and written
by the Spirit the revealer of secrets?"
Maybe the key to these Quaker secrets
lay in the Spirit of God and Christ
and all that I needed to unlock this visionary work
would be to immerse myself in the Spirit,
swallowed-up by God,
losing myself because transformed by the Inward Christ?

Farnsworth observed
"where [the Spirit of God] is manifested,
either male or female … then it is
the man Christ that speaks in them"

I am lost in this language of Man Christ and indwelling God
yet the keys are in my heart and soul as a Quaker.
Why can't I join these 17th century prophets
and be penetrated by the Inward Christ?

Mary Dyer's Hymn

"I am drowning in the past"
—John Berryman,
Homage to Mistress Bradstreet and Other Poems

The Lord came with his power today,
filling up the crisp October day,
playing upon open hearts,
so we sang free together.
Then the Marshall asked finally
aren't you ashamed to walk between these men
but oh no I said
joy erupts inside—I did love our Lord.

That we should come to this hour of death
is not right on the 27th day of
the Lord's 10th month to be hanged.
Our love stays us now.
Declaring to all amidst the noisy drumming
how this became the hour of greatest joy—
no ear can hear like this one—
no tongue can utter joy entire,

no heart can beat such passion.
The soul shall live in everlasting paradise,
commanded of the Lord God himself,
my teacher and guide
and I rejoice in silent hymns of praise
to live in Christ my Father—
shedding blood, I drown and wail.
The Law requires my blood

while I witness and wait in his Power.
A cursed Quaker. I love my husband …

(innocent blood spreads in my veins)
these are not Self-Ends.
The Governor destroys the Holy Seed
with whom life entire is wrapped up.
Were there ever like Laws, heard, here within
people like myself and Fellows

among People who are possessed by
the Christ in the flesh among us?
Hopelessly in thrall, our Enemy pounces
upon us all, now in the name of Boston
to prod the inward Law.
Like Esther and her King,
I am faithful witness,
emanating Joy as the Lord wills.

Coming together against the drums
pricks me hard, blood runs deep
and still they persist in evil.
Hell and blood be done, oh tyrant Boston,
strip these my veins.
His plague be upon you,
all present here at these gallows.
My eyes are clear to the inward Christ.

Richard Waterman's Advice

Beware, O Mary Dyer, banished one, beware
minister Wilson who howls into the night air,
trying on menacing wolfish disguises,
digging special fire-pits as he rises,

determined to root-out subversive error and sin,
tormented by fantasies of deformed births,
imagining poisonous toads covering him,
scampering over Boston Common's earth.

Beware the minister's soul disease
as he proclaims Quaker vanities
caused by deformed wombs and unease.
Turn away from such a man's insanity,

O Mary Dyer, banished one, beware
Minister Wilson's animal howling into the night air.

William Robinson in the Boston Jail

Condemned Quakers wrapped
their flayed skin in blankets,
flies and mosquitos swarm,
no oils from Narragansett healers

no wild ginger for the blood,
no golden seed.
Outside, leaves smoking,
an October moon filtered

through boarded slits
a great-horned owl
who-whoo-whoo,
wood smoke seeps

through battered boards.
A Voice sounds out
yield to His will
like the burning wheel.

William Robinson hears
this song in his rib-cage,
the Lord demanding
not by power, not by strength

but by Spirit.
I will perform through my servant
in whom I delight,
for in Christ's body to die is to gain.

Sing to the Lord,
ungodly Massachusetts.
Give ear and hear
the burning Word of the Lord.

Passageways

William Robinson wheels high into the middle of the air
to be born again on the edges of the great wheel
as this Quaker opens his body in prayer.
William Robinson wheels high into the middle of the air
buoyed up by a channel of voices in midair,
spokes spun around by the Holy Spirit's flywheel.
Robinson wheels high into the middle of the air
to be born again on the edges of the great wheel.

The Wolf Hunter

Dripping hot sticky blood,
the hunter dreamed and felt himself howling aloud
urged by an inner eruption
to join in these songs from the wild darkness,

stained by cries and yowlings,
guttural bursts and riffs from wolves,
their snarling arpeggios rising and falling away
into the dense, humid summertime air

to enter his body and soul, thrusting aside the mind,
penetrating, overflowing with feelings of endless longing.
My grandfather heard inconsolable songs,
cries of despair and tenderness

proclaiming terrible struggle and injustice
yet sublimely muscular
to ring changes like enormous tenor church-bells
calling to this wolf-hunter grandfather

out of the Massachusetts summer night,
modulated by a sliver of ascending moonlight
rising into the nighttime sky
over the great Narraganset Bay.

Wolf-flesh charred
and crackled, rising into the air, spitting out flames
into dreams as wolf bowels
steamed and intestines became ash.

Isaac Penington's Peace

Penington felt a unity of life and death,
sinking down into his soul's seed.
A greenness sprouted from within him afresh.
Penington felt a unity of life and death
as the Lord breathed into his soul and pressed
shining rivulets of grace into his heart.
Penington felt a unity of life and death,
sinking down into his soul's seed.

William Leddra Speaks

This pen trembles as the Lord writes
upon my body in the stillness
to incise his secrets through the Word.
All tastes sweet and smells honey-fused

even with the whip biting my back,
its bloody tracks newly perfumed
as I stand, clanking leg-chains attached to an enormous log.
I watch and wait in the fear of the Lord.

Fear not what these men can do unto me
for I hear a voice within greater than Self.
I am clothed in humility and meekness,
its power swallowing, standing in a faith

that I may—through His favor—
bring all things to the Light
to testify how all is wrought in God.
Through his will, I exhort you, brethren,

enter into wisdom through the Light
to know that by grace we are saved.
Do not trouble yourself about my death
because I have entered into His Kingdom,

glorifying God in this day of Visitation,
yielding to the beloved
to overcome persecution and wickedness
in these perils of the Massachusetts wilderness,

including death itself. Wait
and listen to feel God's love
flow into your vessels
for He who calls us is Holy.

He has prepared a sweet garment to clothe me.
I feel His oil of compassion and love
stitching up my wounds, bringing me
into the house of Salvation.

Ezekiel's Wheel

Ezekiel's wheel spun him round
through a whirlwind, smoking up the fiery air,
swirling higher and higher over Boston Common,

heads of lion, man, ox and eagle
gathered round by the Lord's voice,
skywriting a comet's tail of rage

to light up the noonday clouds
calling out a final cry of Cherubim and Seraphim
breaking up the whirling wheel

as the executioner hooded William Robinson
to swing this Quaker supplicant
far out over Boston

and hundreds of drums became silent
as Ezekiel's wheel spun the Quaker round
through a whirlwind, smoking up the fiery air.

Martyr

Marmaduke Stevenson stood still,
a new earth sprung-up around him,
sprouting fresh, pure grass,
a voice thumped in his chest,
called him to … *ride out of this farm and family*
into Boston's darkness with your light,
oh servant of the Living God.

Sweet words entered his body,
speaking from inside.
He found himself singing hosannas
as Love secreted its way into his bones,
lifting him up from his east Yorkshire plow
to follow this new call,
bringing this Quaker over to Boston,

now as an obedient servant,
cursing Governor Endicott and the General Court
and warning about innocent blood.

The Massachusetts ground trembled,
shaking with the hundreds of drumming soldiers
who accompanied this Quaker to his death.

This Day the Lord has risen up.

William Peddra's Ballad

O' why won't you stay away,
faithful Quaker man
now banished upon pain of death
to be hanged today?

O' why won't you stay away,
now chained and whipped daily,
kept close in darkness and decay
to be hanged today?

O' why won't you stay away
under sure penalty of death the rulers say
but what evil have you done
to be hanged today?

O' why won't you stay away?
You loved those who died, they say,
you proclaimed their innocence, now
to be hanged today?

O' why won't you stay away?
Will you die for breathing the air?
What have they against you
to be hanged today?

O' why won't you stay away,
you write to Friends a day before dying:
my beloved, I wait like a dove
to be hanged today?

O' why won't you stay away,
for at the scaffold you say
take up the cross
to be hanged today?

O' why won't you stay away
as they put the halter round your neck,
Lord Jesus receive my Soul, you say
to be hanged today.

O' why won't you stay away,
faithful Quaker man
now banished upon pain of death
to be hanged today?

O, Mary Dyer

I've done everything I could as a Quaker man.
I prayed to you, holding you and your marriage in the Light.
I sang morning and evening songs
then come-to-Jesus hymns

like "Leaning on the Everlasting Arms" and
"Softly and Tenderly Jesus is Calling," daily
pounding them out on my upright piano,
singing for you, reaching across the centuries.

Should I have burned incense?
Should I have attended Mass and Confession every single day for a
      year?
Should I have fallen on my knees and crawled across the Mojave
      Desert?
Should I have stood on Main Street in Culver City begging for alms?

O, Mary Dyer, after the second banishment from ungodly Massachusetts,
why didn't you stay home with your sweet William
cradled in the loving arms of your family in the midst of Narragansett Bay,
cleaving to the Truth in your heart and soul?

Surely, you knew perfectly well that Massachusetts men
hated you, afraid that your Quaker prophecy would corrupt the common
      people,
threatening the tender bowels of the Bay Colony
because they knew that you carried a deadly disease,

one that disrupted the order of their Divine government
insistent in your devilish pride.
They imagined how you lifted into the October air,
spinning and diving on your pestilential broomstick

like Hecuba entering into Massachusetts.
Why didn't you reject them all and splash your toes

into the Great Bay, digging up chowder clams with your feet,
feeling the tide sliding out even further into the ebbing swirl,

moisture dripping off the clams into the basket
as you waded back home to your family island,
cooking up a mess of clams, beans and corn for your William,
O Mary Dyer?

Writing on the Martyr's Body

Puritan men wrote on her flesh,
this womb that birthed a bloated head,
swelled up fish-like with scales
attended by midwife Anne Hutchinson.

The bowels of hell revealed, diseased.
Her body infused,
this ungoverned woman produced a fetus
with horns, amazing claws

all marks of filth and sin itself
bursting out of her body, Satan's child.
They wrote on Mary Dyer's body
insisting she tremble in fear—

shaking around in a devilish circle
whipping her aging skin
bloody engravings, dripping,

cut into her veins
to draw out bloody droplets
over her wrists, flowing down her arms
trailing onto Boston Common's muddy ground

walking with her into the beginning and the end,
entering into the Lord's paradise.

At the Scaffold

Cursed Quaker, repent and drive the Devil from this Land.
Minister Wilson cajoled Mary Dyer at the scaffold.
She preached the Kingdom of Heaven is at hand.

Do you wish the elders to pray for you?
I desire the prayers of all God's people.
Cursed Quaker, repent and drive the Devil from this Land.

Her Christ-like blood transported new fever,
a body infused with healing faith.
She preached the Kingdom of Heaven is at hand.

She praised God, holding her brethren in her heart,
imagined soaring into the afternoon air.
Cursed Quaker, repent and drive the Devil from this Land.

She longed for her husband and Narragansett Bay
to lay her head on their island's watery home.
She preached the Kingdom of Heaven is at hand.

Father, speak through me thy servant
she cried—I lose my life by finding it here.
Cursed Quaker, repent and drive the Devil from this Land.
She preached the Kingdom of Heaven is at hand.

Return

Thank you, Mary Dyer,
for going out across Long Island Sound
sailing into stiff, southwesterly winds

thank you stranger and pilgrim
to come to Shelter Island's havens of silence
digging clams and oysters all winter.

Thank you for greeting the dying Quaker Southwicks,
there in a winter refuge
as phragmites filled up the shoreline.

Thank you for your love for the Quaker men,
holding them in your heart, those precious brethren,
remembering them dumped into Boston's filth.

Thank you for reaching into winter sunshine
to provide a brief respite before you
entered onto the waves again,

thank you for setting out for the final time
to Boston's scaffold, your soul propelled
in this walk with your Quaker God.

Mary Dyer and Colonel Shaw on Boston Common

The Holy Spirit's breath whispering between them,
martyred Mary Dyer speaks to the Colonel's men,
urging them to ascend to Jesus once again,
chanting songs of the beginning and the end

in a sculptural call and response today.
Mary Dyer sits atop carved Vermont
granite. The Colonel's massive horse prances
across Beacon Street, dancing,

sending a flock of mourning doves rising,
white tail feathers fluttering and diving
around Mary Dyer's immortal hands,
counterpoint to wings of mottled tan.

The bronzed symphony of Colonel Shaw
beats his 54th Black Regiment answer.
A bas-relief Winged Victory hovers over guns
as men march out sharply at a quick-step run.

Whittier's low-relief angel of God model
carries an olive branch into battle
above the etched faces of African-American men
who chant *Omnia Relinquit, Servare Republicam*,

who left everything behind to serve the Republic.
Meanwhile, high on her pedestal, idyllic,
Mary Dyer sits in silence,
her stillness in a meditative pose.

Mourning doves flutter about her frozen hair
cooing a lament into the disappearing air
as I remember what she said near her ending
I am already in paradise.

Acknowledgments

I belong to a vital, growing, spiritually centered Quaker community, the Santa Monica Monthly Meeting in Santa Monica, California. This Quaker spiritual community nurtures my mind, heart and soul and provides a layered, deep container within which – even as a poet – I thrive.

As an artist, I am thankful to participate in multiple Quaker committees and small groups, connected to or started by the Santa Monica community. For years, I have been part of a prayerfully centered "Light Group" (a structured Quaker meditation) with Cynthia Cuza, Monica Faulkner, Rachel Fretz and Ann Fuller; thank you all for such deep listening.

Likewise, as a poet, it helps me to be part of our Adult Education Committee at the Santa Monica Meeting, especially our contemplative reading group and related programs, such a vital process that has included Eleanor Barrett, Mary and Patrick Finn, Laurel Gord, David Neptune, Kim O'Brien, Grayson Schick, Judith Searle, JoAnn Taylor, Gail Thomas and Karsten van Sander.

As part of the Santa Monica Quaker community, I have identified a leading (ministry) in connection with earlier poetry (*Quaker Poems: The Heart Opened*) and have presented some of those poems throughout Southern California at other Quaker Meetings, accompanied by elders, Cynthia Cuza, Rachel Fretz and JoAnn Taylor. We visited and presented poems together at Friends' Meetings in Claremont, Inland Valley, La Jolla, Orange County and Orange Grove Quaker Meetings as well as at my home Meeting in Santa Monica.

For the past year or more, some of these poems were presented at a monthly Poetry Gathering, where we read new poems and offered critique and recommendations; thanks to Rachel Fretz, Ruth Gooley, Loretta Heiser and William Wallis.

I want to thank Mary Klein, editor of *Western Friend*, the official publication of Pacific, North Pacific and Intermountain Yearly Meetings of the

Religious Society of Friends for publishing poems from *Quaker Poems* as well as from *Homage to the Lady with the Dirty Feet and other Vermont Poems* and "At the Scaffold" and "Mary Dyer and Colonel Shaw on Boston Common" from this chapbook. "At the Scaffold" won Honorable Mention in the 2018 Public Poetry "Power" contest.

I wish to note five people who read some of these poems and offered reactions and recommendations. These poet/critics include Michelle Battiste (associated with Black Lawrence Press), David Rigsbee, Rebecca Starks, former editor of *Mud Season Review*, Candellin Wahl, Poetry Co-Editor, *Mud Season Review* and William Wallis, poetry mentor.

In addition, I wish to note Helen Marie Casey's poems about Mary Dyer and other 17th century figures in her chapbook, *Inconsiderate Madness*. Her poems inspired me, and I am in awe of their power and grace.

Finally, I wish to mention a few of the scholars and poets whose work informed these poems. I note Quaker Basil Bunting's poem, "Briggflatts," as well as Seamus Heaney's *Station Island* (with thanks to David Rigsbee for recommending it) as well as John Berryman's poem, "Homage to Mistress Bradstreet." In a variety of ways, my poems drew upon the scholarly work of Anne G. Myles, particularly her work about Mary Dyer, "From Monster to Martyr" in *Early American Literature*, Phyllis Mack's *Visionary Women* and many articles by Carla Pestana, especially "The City upon a Hill under Siege: The Puritan Perception of the Quaker Threat to Massachusetts Bay, 1656-1661" in *The New England Quarterly.* These poems drew upon Joseph Besse's *Quaker Book of Sufferings,* as well. First published in 1643, the reference to Roger Williams, *A Key into the Language of America* is from an edition published by Wayne State University Press, Detroit, 1973.

Thank you to my Quaker wife, Rebecca Warren Searl, for her support of this creative work.

Praise for Mary Dyer's Hymn and Other Quaker Poems

This, for me, is Stanford Searl at his strongest, blending the themes of space, place, and memory, with the theme of Mary Dyer's martyrdom, part of his faith heritage. The collection is poignant and lyrical and yet also apocalyptic in the ways it continually lifts the veil and pulls it aside to reveal another layer of a still more subtle sensibility. This is a collection that for all the Quaker silent prayer is musical and melodic in the way it calls to us. Searl engages past and present, roots and routes, to offer us fresh visions of how we can relate to the confusion of the human condition in our everyday context.

—Ben Pink Dandelion, Professor of Quaker Studies, Woodbrooke

Stanford Searl's tender, lyrical poetry leads us into a past time, arrested, yet brought to life, with mystery and nuance. The harsh receptivity of the Northeast Colonies to anyone not Puritan is laid bare, accompanied by strains of music, sounds of the living marshes, prophecies of my ancient Quaker Mothers of Israel. These courageous souls, neither male nor female in Christ, faithful in the face of hideous persecution challenge my complacency and sometimes tepid engagement with the Spirit. The cruel realities of that fear driven time and place, sadly familiar to our condition today, are juxtaposed with the messages of God's sure presence. The compelling narrative contained in this delicate collection leaves me buoyed up and inspired by the joy and certitude to which these early Friends gave witness. "I am already in Paradise."

—Deborah L. Shaw, Recorded Minister, Director Emeritus of Guilford College's Quaker Leadership Scholars Program

In 1880, John Greenleaf Whittier poetically evoked the sacrifice of Quaker martyrs to the fears and prejudice of the Puritans in "The King's Missive." His verse also captured the continued resilience of those whose "lives preached" in the face of persecution and death. Contemporary Quaker poet Stanford Searl similarly expresses in *Mary Dyer's Hymn and Other Quaker Poems* the poignancy of that time (including Searl's own dissenter ancestry); the witness borne by willing martyrs for a greater cause; and the emotion still experienced by witnesses to such courage and faith. Beyond the stirring poetry and important history, however, are lessons that are still important to learn as latter-day Puritans seek in their own way to take cherished values to the scaffold. Are we willing, like Dyer, Leddra, Stephenson, and Robinson, to face the ultimate sacrifice for a good greater than ourselves? Or are we fated, as another poet (James Russell Lowell in "The Present Crisis") once penned, to see "Truth forever on the scaffold, / Wrong forever on the throne?"

—Max L. Carter, William R. Rogers Director of Friends Center
and Quaker Studies at Guilford College (emeritus)

Stan Searl's exquisite poems give us the powerful feeling of being present with Mary Dyer and the other Quakers, whom the Puritans hanged on Boston Common. He has created a collection of voices, and throughout we feel the beauty of Stan's own singing voice. In this way, these poems are like his other recent book, *Songs for Diana*, a beautiful book of life and love for his daughter.

—Mike Heller, Professor of English Emeritus, Roanoke College,
author of the Pendle Hill Pamphlet *From West Point to Quakerism*

About the Author

Stanford Searl lives in Culver City, California with his wife, Rebecca Warren Searl and is a member of the non-pastoral Santa Monica Monthly Meeting of the Religious Society of Friends (Quakers) in Santa Monica, California. For nearly twenty-five years, Searl was a Core Professor in an interdisciplinary doctoral program at Union Institute & University until the program closed in 2012. He has published two books about Quaker silent worship, including *Voices from the Silence* and *The Meanings of Silence in Quaker Worship*, both published in 2005 and a book of poems, *Quaker Poems: The Heart Opened* in 2014.

In 2016, Foothills Press published his poetry book, *Homage to the Lady with the Dirty Feet and other Vermont Poems* and in early 2019, Kelsay Books published a poetry chapbook, the autobiographical *Songs for Diana*, poems that explore the life and death of his severely handicapped child.

He is working on a new full-length book of poems, *The Cider-Press Man* and other poems of Long Island's North Fork. Details about some of these poems appear on his website, stansearl.com and he is on Facebook as well.

About The Poetry Box®

The Poetry Box® was founded by Shawn Aveningo Sanders & Robert Sanders, who wholeheartedly believe that every day spent with the people you love, doing what you love, is a moment in life worth cherishing. Their boutique press celebrates the talents of their fellow artisans and writers through professional book design and publishing of individual collections, as well as their flagship literary journal, *The Poeming Pigeon®*.

Feel free to visit the online bookstore (thePoetryBox.com), where you'll find more titles including:

November Quilt by Penelope Scambly Schott

Shrinking Bones by Judy K. Mosher

Fireweed by Gudrun Bortman

Psyche's Scroll by Karla Lynn Merrifield

The Poet's Curse by Michael Estabrook

Like the O in Hope by Jeanne Julian

The Unknowable Mystery of Other People by Sally Zakariya

Impossible Ledges by Dianne Avey

Painting the Heart Open by Liz Nakazawa

Bee Dance by Cathy Cain

Small Blue Harbor by Ahrend Torrey

and more . . .